9937

Williamson
Culture and policy

DATE DUE

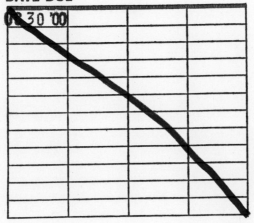

Culture

and

Policy

Culture and

Policy

The United States

and the Hispanic World

by

René de Visme Williamson

Professor of
Political Science
The University of Tennessee

The University of Tennessee Press
Knoxville
1949

To my mother who gave me
my start in Spanish and who
has been one to see the good in
all peoples.

R. W.

Acknowledgment

I am indebted to my colleague, Dr. Lee S. Greene, for encouragement and helpful suggestions, and it is to him that the attractive appearance of the book should be ascribed.

I also want to express my appreciation to Mrs. Virginia Holmes Brown and Mr. Thomas Payne, of The Bureau of Public Administration, for doing a careful and intelligent job of checking and proofreading the manuscript.

R. W.

FOREWORD

On reading, for the second time, Dr. Williamson's penetrating study, I discovered that I was saying very often, "Why did it not occur to me to write this?" Of course, some of the many things that Dr. Williamson has said, and he has said a lot in these few pages, have occurred to me. Some of them I have told my students in lectures, others I have mentioned casually in conversations with friends; most of them I had never been able to set down in a form to be told in a lecture or written down in an article. Fortunately, Dr. Williamson has had the perspicuity to see and the industry to organize and set down on the printed page the many things that all professors of Spanish have always wanted to say.

This is a monograph that one cannot read in a hurry. It is too condensed. Had I been able to organize all this material, I should have used three or four times as many pages. I am sure that Dr. Williamson has made a wise choice in deciding to satisfy himself, and his readers, with the conciseness one finds in his study. As I read I find myself throwing in examples of my own to prove the statements. Let us take the reference to the Spanish beggar.

One day when I was taking my afternoon coffee, a custom that contributes greatly to the Spaniard's enjoyment of life, a beggar touched me on the elbow to ask me for a *perra chica* (penny). Being busy with my conversation, I shook my head and frowned none too politely, I fear. The beggar straightened up in great dignity and would not move on until I took time out to say, "No, thank you; I have nothing for you today." Dr. Williamson, without burdening us with any such illustration, simply points out that the Spanish beggar has the same consciousness of human dignity as the most important man.

Dr. Williamson gives us in his monograph the essence of many books but he does not bother us with the dozens of citations that would serve only to break the train of our thought. He might, for example, have brought as star witnesses to prove the truth of his statements Barrow's *Bible in Spain,* Havelock Ellis' *The Soul of Spain,* or Walter Starkie's *Spanish Raggle Taggle,* to mention only three works of men who knew Spain and Spanish psychology well.

We who have talked and written a bit about Spanish *individualism* will be intrigued and interested, and finally convinced by Dr. Williamson's contention that a better word is *personalism*. It will take careful following of Dr. Williamson's thinking to understand the difference, but it will be a worthwhile experience.

Although it may spoil the story for those who read introductions, I must hasten to say that besides giving us one of the best possible pictures of the Spanish national character, Professor Williamson's monograph has a purpose. To understand Spain is to begin to understand Spanish America; to begin to understand Spanish America is the duty of every citizen of the United States; to understand the Spanish American and to help him to understand us is much more important in the attempt to gain continental solidarity than bribes of ships, money, or movie stars.

JAMES O. SWAIN
Professor of Romance Languages
The University of Tennessee

Such be the sons of Spain,
and strange her fate!
They fight for freedom, who were never free;
A kingless people for a nerveless state,
Her vassals combat when their chieftains flee,
True to the veriest slaves of Treachery;
Fond of a land which gave them naught but life,
Pride points the path that leads to liberty;
Back to the struggle, baffled in the strife,
War, war is still the cry,
"War even to the knife!"

Byron, Childe Harold's Pilgrimage
Canto the First, Verse LXXXVI

HERE are three fundamental reasons for our being interested in Spain and following closely what happens there: (1) Spain is a nation with a very old and rich culture which is well worth knowing for its own sake, (2) Spain occupies a key position geographically which makes her a very important factor in world politics, (3) Spain is the mother country of all the Latin American states—except Brazil and Haiti—which stretch from the Rio Grande to the Tierra del Fuego.

Spain is not a generally known country. Few people possess more than a superficial acquaintance with it, and very rare are those whose knowledge of it is marked by that power of perception and sympathy we call understanding. This is really a peculiar and remarkable fact when you consider that Spain is situated at the confines of western Europe, has a frontage on the Mediterranean and the Atlantic, which have been the two most important maritime arteries of western civilization, and has filled most of South America and a sizable portion of North America with her language, culture, and institutions. No less remarkable is the profound indifference of most Spaniards for that fact.

The Peculiarities of Spanish Nationalism and Their Basis in Spanish National Character

THIS indifference should not be interpreted to mean that the Spanish people are devoid of nationalism but rather that they, like all other peoples, have developed a brand of their own in conformity with the requirements of their national character. Spanish nationalism is unique in that it lacks the usual aggressiveness which insists that other nations should either adopt one's own national culture or else accept an inferior position. The Spaniard does not strut like the German for his *Kultur,* he is free of the Englishman's irritating tacit assumption that he is entitled to the same treatment abroad that he would get at home, he does not claim that his country is the fountainhead of cultural enlightenment and civilization as does the typical French nationalist, and he will not bother to match superlatives with the American about who has the biggest and best of anything. He is not interested in the claims of others and feels no urge to press his own on anybody else. One might like to characterize Spanish nationalism as "insular" were it not for the obvious fact that Spain is not an island—which is probably just as well since the word might suggest misleading resemblances with the English brand. Whereas the Englishman looks at the world from a distance across the water and talks about the "other side" of everything, the Spaniard looks not at but over the world from the heights of his mountain or plateau and it would never occur to him that there are "two sides" to everything. The Englishman is famous for his inclination to keep his distance, and he gets very distant indeed when forced to deal with somebody he disapproves of or dislikes. On the other hand, the Spaniard might be said to keep his altitude and he gets more and more aloof as his disapproval becomes greater. There is an undeniable quality of separateness about the Spaniard, and his French neighbors have recognized it in their none-too-friendly saying that "Europe ends at the Pyrenees."

Although there does exist a thing called "Spanish nationalism," the adequacy of the name is open to question. The accepted concept of a nation is not well suited to Spanish conditions and must be handled with care lest it run afoul of regional sensitiveness. The difficulty is caused mainly by the Catalonians and the Basques both of whom consider that they themselves are nations in the full sense of the term, and there are other provinces like Galicia in which popular sentiment has been developing along similar lines. The one thing which makes the word acceptable, though still dangerous, is the practice of calling it Spanish. It happens that usage has imparted a rather low emotional voltage to the word "Spain." Intrinsically a geographic term, it possesses the inestimable virtue of being politically neutral and is the only possible common denominator in a country afflicted by diverse centrifugal regionalisms. "Iberic" is unacceptable because of Portugal, and "Hispanic" is disqualified on account of its inclusion of the Spanish speaking peoples of Latin America. The words "Spain" and "Spanish,"

4.

therefore, derive their real significance from what they avoid and not what they identify. Thus, the Spaniards will say that their language is Spanish when the truth is that it is Castilian, but they know that this is one of those truths that is not good to be told. The consequence is that it is permissible to refer to "Spanish nationalism," provided one remembers its intentionally negative and evasive character whose function is that of a political shock absorber. How far this concept deviates from the ordinary conventional one is too apparent to require demonstration. It is regrettable, however, that established usage does not sanction the expression "Spanish pride" as a substitute, for it would be much truer—and in a far deeper sense—than the denatured one which is now current.

There is probably more pride in a Spanish beggar than is likely to be encountered among English lords and American captains of industry, and his dignity is so great that even his rags are somehow not without a certain touch of majesty. American businessmen who are accustomed to all "the advantages" an industrial civilization can confer would find it astounding and utterly incomprehensible. What, they would want to know, has this Spanish beggar to be proud about? I think a Spaniard would answer approximately thus: the burning spark of the human spirit besides which political prestige, military power, and material wealth pale into insignificance! This pride harmonizes very nicely with the kind of politeness one finds in Spain and probably accounts for its distinctive character. Spanish politeness is full of set phrases and fixed formulae (e.g., "Your dependable servant who kisses your hands"—or your feet, in the case of a lady) which are used even in business correspondence. It is a formal, elaborate, and ornate manner which is, nevertheless, free from the slightest trace of obsequiousness or servile spirit and which seems least out of place when it is found in association with the old-fashioned virtues such as hospitality and liberality, and Spain is exactly the place where they are still quite common. Liberality, for instance, is not just an old word for generosity because it means knowing how to be generous, which implies the presence of genuinely unselfish good will in motivation and the habitual use of intelligence in action instead of a mere separation between the giver and the gift. It comes close to being largesse when it is exercised by a person of ample means in a free and uncalculating way. Spanish politeness has exactly that feel of liberality about it and reflects the unspoken premise that no man is too poor to be liberal with his compliments.

This blending or partial fusion of politeness, liberality, and pride is a peculiarly Spanish trait, and evidences of it may be found at innumerable little points in everyday life. The current use of words like *caballero* and *don* in conversation, which carries an implied compliment, has the same significance that the word "Sir" would have in England if its use were extended to every man instead of being restricted as it is now to those who have been knighted by the King and those who have a legal right to the rank of baronet. *Señor* may mean either man or God (with a capital "S" in the latter case). The Spanish equivalent for "you" is *Vd.* which is a contraction of *Usted* which, in turn, is itself a contraction of *Vuestra Merced* ("your mercy" or "your grace"), and the first letter is capitalized and thus constitutes the one Spanish departure from French usage concerning capital letters. When it comes to the matter of word-building by accretion, as one might say, which consists in making a new word by combining several old ones, a comparison between German and Spanish is interesting. The Germans are famous for this word-building process. They may and frequently do use it for all names except proper names (though aristocratic names are an exception to the exception and, therefore, a special privilege for a few people). Spanish usage, however, is the exact reverse of the German: proper names are the only instance when it is permissible, and it makes no difference whether they are aristocratic names or not. A man who likes his mother's maiden name simply puts it after his own so that time and usage will link them as though they were connected by a hyphen. If a Mr. Fulano Sánchez likes his mother's maiden name of García, he can become Mr. Fulano Sánchez García. If his son Juan wants to make another change he can be Mr. Juan Sánchez. He may also decide to remain Mr. Juan Sánchez García. But he might like the maiden name of his own mother as well as his grandmother's, in which case he may call himself Mr. Juan Sánchez García y Castillo. This process of picking up names every generation can go on indefinitely and is open to all, but it is the aristocracy which is most likely to carry it to the greatest—and sometimes absurd— lengths. There is a story to the effect that a Spanish nobleman arrived at a small French inn very late one night and knocked on the door until the innkeeper woke up and, leaning out of the window into the dark, asked who was knocking. The Spaniard immediately launched forth with a recital of all his names, whereupon the French innkeeper said he had not enough room for that many people and went back to bed without opening the door.

Spanish hospitality likewise reflects this peculiar combination of qualities. If a guest says something nice about the house where he is staying, his Spanish host will immediately say: "This is your house"—metaphorically, of course. But he will not say that it is a trifle or a mere nothing as I understand the custom is among the Chinese. Nothing personal is ever a trifling matter to a Spaniard. Neither will he follow the American practice of urging his guest to "make himself at home." Why should he? He has already shot his bolt, so to speak, and gone as far as it is possible to go when he said it is "your house." Adding anything more would be superfluous or would even detract from his original statement by casting doubt upon its genuineness.

All these language habits, social forms, national customs, and popular attitudes indicate the enormously high value which the Spanish place on the individual human being and a strik-

ingly deep belief in equality. On the other hand, the existence
of a great and sometimes shocking degree of inequality as it is
embodied in the titled aristocracy and the economically privi-
leged is also an indisputable fact. Since this inequality is an
artificially imposed and maintained condition whose explanation
must be sought in the present and past politics of the country,
it would be truer to say that the basic national values are
flouted rather than disproved. The national conviction and feeling that the individual human being is the highest value in life
and that it applies to all men equally from beggar to prince must
be recognized as having a much more pervasive power and an
infinitely stronger basis. Constitutions, kings, economic organizations, wars, revolutions, and conquests come and go, but
basic national values woven into the very stuff and substance of
everyday life survive them all. They may be violated up to a
certain point—sometimes none-too-certain—but never totally.
In fact, abiding by them in most cases is the price exacted for
departing from them in some cases. In their official capacity
the followers of General Franco do not act in a manner con-
sistent with the national emphasis on the value of the individual,
and still less do they show any respect for equality. In spite of
this, however, they are by no means completely free agents.
Anyone who doubts it should ask himself what would happen
if Franco and his followers, who flout national values in the
political and economic realism, tried to flout them as they are
embodied in the nation's folkways, language, taste, family life,
and standards of courteous behavior. They could never "get
away" with that sort of conduct and, being after all Spaniards,
the probabilities are that they would not want to make any
such attempt. The desire to flout national values thoroughly
and consistently in every walk of life from the government to
individual households and from the laws of the land to the
rules of grammar and the standards of correct literary style
could scarcely be expected from anybody except foreigners.
The few who took a stab at it did not last long nor did they

find the going pleasant and smooth while they lasted. Napoleon himself with all his power and prestige couldn't do it.

This brings us back, therefore, to the attitude toward the individual human being which is implicit in Spanish life. It would be easy to conclude from this attitude that the Spanish nation is inherently democratic, for the sacredness and equality of men are certainly the indispensable foundation of democracy. Nevertheless, it would be a questionable conclusion, even though it is quite probable that the Spaniards could learn to develop and operate a democratic form of government very successfully. The thing which makes the natural affinity of the Spanish people for democratic government doubtful or at least debatable is that democracy is demo*cracy,* which means the rule of the people. Now it is precisely this business of ruling which the Spaniards find distasteful, and if it were removed from democracy the remainder would be nothing other than anarchism. It should not surprise anyone, there-fore, to discover that there are people who say that the Spaniard is by nature an anarchist. Count Carlo Sforza, the well-known and distinguished Italian statesman, once quoted some remarks made to him by the late King Alfonso XIII on this very point. According to Sforza, the King said: "Are Italians as contrary to any form of govern-ment as Spaniards? In Italy the first word a baby says is 'Mama,' and if they are very clever, they may say 'Papa.' But here in Spain the first word of any boy is 'No.'"[1] If we look at Spanish individualism a little more closely, it will be-come apparent that the word "individualism" does not fit any too well either. As was true with "nation," so it is in this case. The difficulty is caused by the attempt to apply to Spain a concept which was developed in a foreign background where it acquired particular associations and shades of mean-ing. As we think of it, "individualism" may mean a specific

---

[1] Carlo Sforza, "The Diplomatic Debacle: London and Paris Before Mu-nich," *The Annals of the American Academy of Political and Social Science,* 218 (November, 1941), 40.

economic system corresponding fairly closely with capitalism in its earlier stages, or we might be referring to a political system in which individuals possess definite civil rights enumerated in a constitution and enforced by the courts, or we could be using it in a philosophical sense as being the opposite of collectivism and making "individual" more or less synonymous with "type" or "unit." None of these meanings fits in with what the Spaniard has in mind. He is not thinking about anything economic—especially not a system of any kind. Neither is he thinking about rights or their possession, and concepts like "type" and "unit" are the very negation of what he believes in. His idea is entirely different from all this. It isn't how a living may be earned that he thinks important, but who earns it. It isn't what legal rights you happen to have that he wants to know about but who you are. It isn't what a human being has which can be duplicated in every other human being which deeply concerns him but rather what any one human being has that is unique and distinctive. In short, the central and supreme national value of Spain is a person and not an individual. There is a word in Spanish for the doctrine which takes that position, namely, *personalismo*. The easiest way to render it into English, of course, is to give it the slavishly literal and very obvious translation of personalism, but this is merely a verbal trick to which the response is a characteristic blank. It is just an empty shell or mould, but its simplicity and the lack of any alternative make it advisable to use the word "personalism" provided a definite content is poured into it to give it substance.

ꙅINCE there exists a close connection between the concept of personalism and the geographic environmental context in which it was developed, a helpful way of attacking the problem is to approach it from the angle of Spain's physical characteristics with special emphasis on Castile.

Most of Spain is a high arid plateau which is difficult of access in practically every sense: it is hard to get into it, it is hard to get out of it, and it is hard to get around in it. To the north it is sealed off by the Pyrenees which form a formidable and almost impassable barrier not so much because they are among the highest mountains in Europe but because they rise like a huge perpendicular wall with scarcely any passes or other breaks. On all other sides Spain is surrounded by water (except for Portugal, of course). The whole peninsula is cut through by a series of mountain ranges, usually high and invariably rough, running in a general east and west direction right into the sea where they present their narrow edges instead of their sides to the shore. The result is that there are not many good ports and the coastal towns have only a short triangular plain behind them and very poor communications with either the hinterland or each other. Most of the Spanish coast looks as if the mythical Hercules had gone around the shore driving a number of wedges of various sizes into the cliffs, thus leaving a good many dents some of which are so small that there is room for only one tiny fishing village in them. These same mountains also make traveling inland from one province to another an arduous enterprise. The rivers are even worse an obstacle, if possible. You cannot navigate them for the excellent reason that most of them are dry for the greater part of the year or boast of a thin trickle of water, and anyone who tried to navigate them during the exceptional time when the water is more plentiful would soon have his boat smashed to bits. On the other hand, these rivers cut through deep canyons and gorges. This means that you cannot throw a bridge over them easily because they are too wide across the top, and neither can you ford them because the steep and often precipitous banks discourage attempts to get to the bottom. The natural obstacles and complications hindering travel are so numerous and diverse—one is tempted to say "ingenious"— that they look like the work of some evil spirit who did it on purpose to condemn the inhabitants to isolation and separatism. Indeed, Spain has been compared to a trap which few people enter and which practically no one leaves. From a military point of view Spain is an ideal place for the purpose of slowing down, immobilizing, grinding up, and wearing out armies. It is worth noting that the Allies and the Axis both gave it a wide berth during World War II.

At the heart and center of that natural fortress which is Spain lie the two provinces of Old and New Castile where the politically dominant power in Spain is located. Castile is a very high plateau—in fact, in all Europe it is only in Switzerland that the average elevation is greater. It is a hot, dry, rocky, and barren place. There never were many trees there on account of the moisture deficiency, but the greater part of those few that managed to survive the climate did not survive the Castilians who completed the job of denuding the country. Castilians seem to suffer from a peculiar kind of outdoor claustrophobia, judging by the explanations some of them give for hating trees—e.g., that they like long unobstructed vistas, that the trees give them an oppressive feeling of confinement and being hemmed in, that too much green affects them the way a cup of coffee would if somebody emptied the whole sugar bowl into it. Their feeling is very understandable to someone who has seen Castile with his own eyes.

Castile is a place bathed in a luminous and transparent atmosphere enabling the eye to see for vast distances. It impresses one with an overwhelming feeling of being alone in the world.

12.

There seems to be a superabundance of sky which induces in the onlooker a sense of awe at the immensity of pure uninhabited space. But this land so full of solitude, spaciousness, and silence evokes no sense of peace, for it is a violent country. The ground looks as though it had had convulsions, much of it is a chaos of rocks lying under a sky of brass so hot that it looks more white than blue, and the general coloring of the landscape is sometimes brilliant, always austere, never restful, with greys, yellows, and reds predominating. After a long and merciless beating from the rays of a blistering sun, the jagged hills of bare rock begin to radiate heat as the day draws to a close so that, for a while, the land looks as though a halo were resting on its brow. It is also a pitiless and exhausting country in which men must go up and down and around uncompromisingly rugged ground that feels as hot as if it were being consumed by a raging fever, a country where men must endure a light so intense that the glare is likely to cause eye trouble if the dust hasn't already done so and to inflict a fatigue that feels more like pain, a country in which men must exert themselves in an atmosphere so dry that it dehydrates you as you breathe. It is an inhospitable and ungenerous country where men have to struggle hard to squeeze a meagre subsistence from a poor, thin, and sandy soil abandoned among great chunks of rock and forlorn-looking salt beds of gleaming white. Some of the foreigners who hear about this strange country and some of those who have visited it marvel that anybody should be willing to live there and feel that they can readily understand why Pizarro and Cortés and others left home. Yet that reaction proves that they don't know how the Castilians (and those other Spaniards whose section is similar) feel about their native land. One conclusive and obvious proof that the reaction is thoroughly wrong is that those Spaniards who left Spain to go to the Americas sought out wherever possible those very places in the New World which most closely resembled the land of their birth.

It would be an unnatural thing, in a country with these physical characteristics, if the inhabitants lived in widely scattered farm houses. No one should be surprised, therefore, to learn that the Castilians live in cities and towns. The typical Castilian city, however, has a very special and original stamp as does nearly everything else in that country. It is practically always a natural fortress located in a site nothing short of spectacular and further re-enforced by man-made fortifications. It stands high up in a virtually impregnable position, seemingly reaching for the skies, dominating a vast expanse that can look as desolate as the moon. The city of Segovia, for example, is perched on a huge more or less triangular rock that juts out like a promontory into space, surrounded by a chasm or canyon dug narrow and deep by two torrents, walled in by a thick stone rampart following the edge of the precipice, and kept supplied with water by a stately aqueduct built under the Roman emperor Trajan out of massive blocks of granite held together without cement by their sheer weight. Two spires rise above the roofs of the city: one is that of a magnificent old cathedral, and the other belongs to that combination of castle and fort the Spanish call *Alcázar* which stands on one point of the triangle overlooking the deepest and steepest part of the canyon where the two torrents merge.

Now it is possible to look back over this Castilian environment and see how very much it has to do with personalism. It is a country in which people must of necessity be tough and strong. The dispersal of the cities and towns over the Castilian plateau together with the bad communications meant that in a preindustrial age that toughness and strength would have to take the form of individual (or at most local) self-reliance rather than dependence on a large collective organization. If there was to be some sort of protection against the Moors or other invaders, the people would have to supply it for themselves because the long arm of the monarchy with its supporting armies and bureaucrats would have great trouble reaching them

14.

either to defend or oppress them. The poverty of the land called for pastoral and farming activities which forced a daily dispersal over the countryside. This meant that the men would sally forth from the city each morning and return each evening, thus imparting to city life the character of a great pulse geared to the natural rhythm of diurnal and seasonal change. That a man should go out alone each day and return each night to find in his family's affection moral protection against extreme loneliness and to enjoy within the walls of his home and city physical protection against alien enemies was bound to have a tremendous formative influence, and that influence was such as to give the whole of existence a strongly personal aspect. This fundamental and immemorial rhythm permeates Spanish life on all levels. Just as the ordinary Castilian sallies forth in the solitary silent alien world to seek a living unregimented by government and unhampered by other men, so did the Cid Campeador to liberate his country from the yoke of the Moor, so did Don Quixote to live the ideals of chivalry, so did Pizarro and Cortés to conquer a new empire for their King and amass glory and gold for themselves, so did Ponce de León to find the Fountain of Youth, so did many Spanish missionaries to convert the Indians to Christianity, so did Ignatius Loyola to win Protestant Europe back to Catholicism. All these and countless other Spaniards did essentially the same thing in essentially the same way, i.e., a personal way, going singly or in small groups where leadership could remain personal, preferably where there was plenty of vacant space around them as a further guarantee of independence.

The Spaniard's return, however, is just as noteworthy as his departure. In faithful conformity with the basic ancestral rhythmical pattern of Castilian life, his every trip is a round trip. Like those two technically foreign but spiritually Spanish explorers, Columbus and Magellan, he considers that even a journey of world-wide dimensions is not concluded by reaching his destination but by returning home. It is interesting to observe that there are two Europeans whose homes are said to be their castles: the Englishman and the Spaniard. As might be expected, however, the similarity is quite superficial and accidental. To say that an Englishman's home is his castle means that the law of the land recognizes his right to privacy and seclusion, and that the whole machinery of government stands ready to defend it against the whole world. It is otherwise with the Spaniard. In the first place, to be strictly true to life, it would be better to say that the Spaniard's castle is his home rather than the other way around. By its strategic location and its construction the castle is itself the right to privacy and seclusion materialized into rock—by a kind of political trans-substantiation, as it were—and it is also the perfectly obvious guarantee of that right against all comers, including even the government itself. The castle, therefore, is the external symbol of the Spaniard's passion for personal independence.

Whoever is responsible for the well-known expression "to build a castle in Spain" was the victim of a serious misunderstanding, for what could be more tangible and less imaginary than rock? Perhaps the origin of this misunderstanding was the story of Don Quixote's immortal error when he mistook an inn for a castle. But this would be going from bad to worse. After all, Don Quixote was a legendary character whose greatness is due to the fact that he externalized in his exploits the latent tendencies of his countrymen. Like all forms of art, literature gets at the inner realities of life by giving expression to what is ordinarily unexpressed or even possibly inexpressible and makes these realities visible by exaggerating them. What, then, was the latent inner reality to which Don Quixote was giving an exaggerated expression when he made that mistake? It was the instinctive assumption that this human world is a world of castles, that every *casa* (house) is spiritually a *castillo* (castle). It was also an expression of the Spaniard's inner aversion to what is public or for hire. The idea of *res nullius* denoting a thing which belongs to nobody, which animated the British settlers in America and the American westward movement, doesn't come naturally to the Spaniard. To him the word "public" means "impersonal," and that is why he doesn't like it. He avoided it as much as possible. Land which did not belong to the individual Spaniard but which was used for public purposes belonged to the King (who is a person) and not to "the State" (which is an abstraction), and where the land was obviously unwanted and unclaimed by anybody, he thought of it as belonging to God (who is a Person too). When the Catholic church had acquired such large possessions that the entire Spanish economy was affected, he gave this subtraction from the national domain the significant name of *mano muerta* (the dead hand)—and only persons have hands. In view of all these facts, the supposition that every house is a castle is not so far-fetched after all, especially in a country named *Castilla* which means "land of castles."

To say that the Spaniard's castle is his home is, of course, a metaphorical way of speaking, but it is not one whit more so than the conventional reference to the Englishman's home. Every private residence and dwelling place isn't literally a castle in England any more than it is in Spain—it could be a hut, hovel, shack, bungalow, cottage, mansion, or palace. The point is not what it is physically but how one looks at it. The Englishman, with his people's uncanny ability to navigate through life by leaving obstacles shrouded in a convenient semi-darkness and to move forward successfully on a course strewn with by-passed and unsolved problems, has adopted the ambiguous word of "home." Sometimes "home" means "house" and sometimes not. It has whichever meaning happens to suit the Englishman's purpose at the moment. It can refer equally well to the moral unity of a family tied by spiritual bonds, or to the physical setting which a family has to have to serve material needs of existence. A home is a house, and then it isn't one! But which is true? Here the Englishman—probably with an expression of surprised candor—will un-

doubtedly reply: "Why, they are both true, of course!" It
was a son of the Mediterranean civilization who cut the Gor-
dian knot. Had he been an Englishman, he would very simply
have walked away.

The Spaniard meets the situation full tilt (and if he does
strike a windmill once in a while, what of it?). He meets
it in a way which, for him, is completely characteristic: he
spiritualizes the house. A home is a *casa* (house), definitely.
The family is the only human institution in which human relations are fully personal, and a house is the physical structure
whose protective walls cut off impersonal and therefore alien
intrusions. The Spanish word for getting married, *casarse,*
is highly significant: it means "to put oneself into a house,"
hence a married woman is *casada* (housed in). It is also worth
noting that a married man is also *casado* (for the Spanish
language does not have the ambiguous possibilities of English
whereby a man can have an illicit date with a "cousin" or a
"friend" and say so with perfect verbal sincerity and possible
impunity). To English or American ears, however, "housed
in" sounds dreadfully like "imprisoned" or "locked up." For
them it would be a hateful way of putting it, though there is
probably no dearth of women in this country who would feel
that it is all-too-true.

o understand the full meaning of *personalismo*, however, the geographic basis is not enough. There are
certain aspects of it, notably its antistate if not antisocial
slant, whose origin is more historical than anything else. The
history of Spain has been punctuated at several important
points by the intrusion of foreign elements which took possession of the government and imposed what was essentially
a foreign rule on the country. Tragic is perhaps not too
strong a word to designate Spain's misfortune of having had
her people repeatedly robbed of the control of their own destiny. The imposition and establishment of General Franco's
rule by Hitler and Mussolini is only the latest instance of
this misfortune. It began with the Moors who were alien in
religion as well as in race. It took the Spanish about eight
centuries to get rid of them.

The next instance of it came with Charles V. It is true
that he had a legitimate claim to the throne through his mother
and was therefore King by right of inheritance, which was
something every Spaniard could understand. But it is also
true that he was personally a German in speech and background,
hence a foreigner. Furthermore, he continued to rule Austria
and the Low Countries as well as Spain. Although history
does record a number of cases in which foreign monarchs
completely espoused the interest and welfare of their adopted
subjects, it must be remembered that in every case their success as rulers was linked wholly to the fortunes of their people. This was not so with Charles V because his interest
was divided between his Germanic and Hispanic subjects.
Moreover, he brought in with him many foreign officials (uni-
formly called "Flemish" by the Spaniards) who spread themselves over the country like a bevy of carpetbaggers. Naturally,
this was bitterly resented by the Spaniards and led to a re-

bellion in Castile. This rebellion, which is known to Spanish historians as *la Guerra de las Communidades* ("the War of the Communities"), is another one of those things which has been unknown, ignored, or barely noticed outside of Spain. Even in Spain it has not been given the emphasis it deserves. The rebellion was not a mass uprising of the Spanish people resorting to arms as though by common accord to eject the foreign intruders but was rather the armed resistance of some Spanish people acting separately and independently in their natural fortresses that dot the land of Castile. It is also significant that the centers of resistance were named "communities" and not "cities." This was because the really important and salient fact about these cities was that they were small enough to be spiritual as well as physical entities in which individual relations could be on the personal level, and it was this underlying reality which made them centers of resistance. As usually happens when an aggressor is permitted to meet scattered and uncoordinated resistance with concentrated forces favored by the choice of time and place, the aggressor won out and Charles V began what the Spaniards have called, perhaps ironically, *El Siglo de Oro* ("the Century of Gold"). Spanish culture eventually acted like a powerful solvent on this alien Germanic rule and assimilated Charles' son, Philip II, who left to posterity a tangible evidence of this triumph of the Castilian spirit in the form of the Escorial, a monastery whose massive strength and austere lines perfectly symbolized the characteristically Castilian fusion of military and religious spirits. Nevertheless, the victory was not won without cost, and there are those who believe that with the loss of the War of the Communities something went out of the Spanish soul never to return again.

In any event, this was not to be the last cruel blow to Spanish pride. There came the War of the Spanish Succession which was concluded by the accession of Philip V, grandson of Louis XIV, who brought down more foreign officials—

French, this time. This alien spirit also left a memorial of stone in the form of the Little Trianon palace which is a bit of France in the heart of Spain. Still later, there followed the spectacular failure of Napoleon to impose his brother Joseph as King of Spain, then a brief and ineffectual transplanting of the Italian House of Savoy, then an abortive attempt to put a Hohenzollern on the Spanish throne around 1870, and finally the brutal conquest of Spain by Hitler and Mussolini, crudely and imperfectly, veiled behind the pasty-faced and mediocre Spanish commander of Moorish troops, the corpulent General Francisco Franco.

And what prospect is there in store for the unfortunate people of Spain? Will the coming demise of the dictatorship of the Nazi-Fascist caretaker be followed by a new monarch by the Grace of London, Wall Street, and the United States Department of State? Or will a stupid and short-sighted policy by the western democracies once again betray their friends by driving an unwilling Spanish people into the bearish clasp of the Kremlin so that Joseph Stalin might set up a new dictatorship and inflict upon the helpless Spaniards with the Hammer and the Sickle the longest and harshest beating they have received since the one under the Moorish Crescent? Or will the Spanish people get a chance to establish their own national government and to take the control of their own affairs into their own hands, that they might work out their own destiny independently of the capitalist democracies of the West and the communist dictatorships of the East?

IT is this historical background which best explains the profound alienation of the Spanish people from their government and their cynical indifference to the vicissitudes of Spanish politics, making them virtually foreigners in their own country. The effects on the government were no less marked. Governments derive their strength from the depth of their roots in the population they govern, their stability is as great as their base is broad, and their voice is loud and authoritative when the great masses function like a sounding board and give that voice magnitude and volume. These are the necessary conditions of healthy governments regardless of constitutional forms. The Spanish people have destroyed these conditions by their aloof indifference which amounts to a silent daily repudiation of their government. As a consequence, whatever the government does is denatured and turns sour in the very doing of it, as though an evil spell had been cast upon it. Great organizations, such as General Primo de Rivera's *Unión Patriótica* was intended to be, are dismal and ghost-like failures when nobody will join them. When a demonstration is staged to make a show of strength designed to impress domestic and foreign opinion, the impression produced is pitiful because it is so painfully apparent to everybody that there is no popular determination to follow through; hence the whole undertaking looks like exactly what it is, an unspeakably sorry bluff. Great speeches and solemn pronouncements are cursed with a hollow and derisive ring because it is so glaringly obvious that they evoke no response—no hearts beat faster, no heads nod in silent assent, no eyes shine brighter, no voices are lifted either to curse or to cheer. Everything the government does is stillborn or is so immediately ineffectual that it would have been preferable never to have tried at all.

A government thus forsaken by its people is unstable because its base is too narrow, too small, too much on the same pattern. It tends to be monopolized by an office-holding class of professional politicians who are monotonously alike in their habits, viewpoints, interests, and ambitions. There is a natural psychological selection at work which has a narrowing effect, and the effect is even more pronounced when there is an ideological selection as well. What this class lacks most of all, therefore, are the natural correctives which could come only from fellow-citizens who belong to different regions, classes, and professions. Stability, progress, and strength are to be found where there is a diversity of types and groups working for common ends, and it is this diversity which permits the pooling of a wide range of mutually complementary human resources and the canceling out of individual and group defects. A monopoly of the government by an office-holding class of professional politicians means the rule of incompetent leaders supported by a scanty and lightweight following, unrestrained by principles, and abandoned to the shifty and unstable courses that go with expediency and opportunism. The traditional processes of parliamentary government like votes of confidence, the reshuffling of Cabinets, the calling of general elections, become a mockery. The more spectacular processes of dictatorships and revolutionary movements are similarly denatured and blighted. Revolutions are reduced to "palace revolutions," conspiracies, and cabals which are more closely related to the musical opera than to actual life. The stature of generals, which they themselves would doubtless like to think is of Napoleonic dimensions, is shrunk in size to such a degree that they look more like noisy and puny bantam roosters. A rapid succession of Prime Ministers without a parliamentary majority, Presidents without a popular following, generals without an army dominate the scene and the body politic is about to die of boredom and ridicule.

This appalling situation is the usual revenge of the Spanish people for the deadly damage done to their pride and their persons by the imposition of foreign rule. Moreover, this rule has been foreign in a much deeper sense than the alien national origins and background of some of the rulers who, after all, were not numerous if the whole span of Spanish history be considered. It was foreign because it did violence to the deep underlying feeling of the Spanish people for the sacredness of human personality belonging equally to all men. The circumstance that the rulers might be native Spaniards does not make this rule less foreign. The alienation of the Spanish people was the price which government paid for imposing and maintaining social inequality, economic privilege, and political favoritism in defiance of the national sense of right. It was a solemn disavowal so universal and so strong that it was like a national conspiracy which needed neither plot nor other prearrangement in order to exist, and so deep that it became a habit which the Spanish colonists took to America with them where it has had the political results that are familiar to us.

This historical evolution in the direction of political apathy, superimposed as it has been on the natural tendency of the geographic environment to foster separatism and on the similarly oriented influence of a very largely preindustrial economy, was all that was necessary to give the finishing touches to one of Spain's most striking peculiarities; namely, a certain amorphous quality or shapelessness which the Spanish philosopher José Ortega y Gasset has characterized as invertebrate. Ortega's word is rather well chosen, for the principal mark of invertebrate organisms is that they have little or no differentiation of structure so that the cells continue to live more or less independently with scarcely any connection between them except physical proximity. A like situation may be said to exist in social organisms such as a nation when the only relations within it are personal relations between individuals. It is evident, of course, that there is no such thing as a social "organism" in a strict sense and that no human society can be absolutely and purely invertebrate, but some societies lean more in that direction than others and the Spanish nation is assuredly one of those that do. In Spain the family is the only social institution involving human relations, other than the personal ones, which can be said to have any real strength. With the exception of two and possibly three regions, social institutions like labor unions and business corporations are embryonic. There is little economic differentiation because most Spaniards have not learned and apparently do not want to organize themselves in reasonably enduring associations for the purpose of controlling prices, wages, production, conditions of labor, and so on. These matters are very largely dealt with on a person to person basis. I remember the words of a Basque priest who was sitting next to me as we were riding through Castile in a bus. He was looking at wheat being thrashed by the tramping of a little donkey moving in a circle and, with an expression of disgust, he said: "That's the way they were doing it in Jesus Christ's day!" These words could be applied to a good many things economic in Spain without being far wrong. A similar prevalence of personal factors is typical of political life. In most countries the existence of political parties means that large numbers of individuals have formed relatively permanent ties along ideological, economic, and sectional lines for the purpose of encouraging certain governmental activities and restraining others. Political parties cause an appreciable differentiation of the population by splitting it into general and loosely knit groups such as conservatives, liberals, nationalists, and socialists. There were many political parties in pre-Franco Spain, it is true, but their nature was such as to underscore the unwillingness of the Spaniards to get away from what is personal. The hold of these parties over the electorate was weak and uncertain in some parts of the country and practically nonexistent in other parts, which fact therefore tended to show that whatever differentiation took place applied to a relatively small number of persons interested in politics rather than to the population as a whole which continued as undifferentiated as ever. That meant weakness since governments are not apt to be much impressed by the support or the opposition of parties so incapable of bringing pressure to bear on them. The number of parties and the lack of discipline within them were further evidence of the extreme reluctance of Spaniards to subordinate person to party, and attempts to ignore it were met by expulsions, secessions, and splits. Party politics on the highest national level, therefore, was pretty largely the personal rivalries and personal following among small cliques operating under deceptive labels and with negligible popular support. Dictators like Rivera and Franco had far less trouble eliminating these anaemic political parties than they did when they tried to organize one of their own, which ought not to be surprising since they were going with the grain in the first instance but against it in the second. The Catholic church might have been the one exception to this situation, but the indications are that it has suffered the same alienation from the people as the government, and for much the same reason.

The degree to which any given country properly can be said to be invertebrate or amorphous varies directly with the extent to which some people can answer for a much larger number of people in the various fields of human endeavor. Is there a political party organization which can either predict or control the vote of any particular section or class grouping in a general election? Are there labor leaders who can guarantee in advance what their union members will think and do on any particular question? Are there business associations or organizations whose leaders may rightly be considered the spokesmen of a sizable and determinate number of businessmen on certain definite topics? If these questions can be answered in the affirmative, the country is not invertebrate or amorphous but, on the contrary, is highly differentiated and organized. If the answer be negative, however, public opinion on any particular subject is chiefly a fortuitous coincidence or individual opinions which can be ascertained better by the methods of statistics than by those of representation.

The Spanish Guerrilla: War on the Personal Level

SPANISH personalism is also revealed in another form of resistance to illegitimate authority which is known by the significantly Spanish name of *guerrilla*. If one follows the rules of grammar, guerrilla means "little war" because it is the diminutive form of *guerra* (war). But this is a case where political reality and grammatical requirements are incompatible, the same sort of incompatibility being involved here which we encounter when we say "the United States is" in defiance of the rules of grammar which require that a plural verb be used with a plural subject. A guerrilla is not necessarily a "little war" at all, as Napoleon would undoubtedly be willing to testify if he could. It is really war conducted by individuals fighting independently, i.e., war on the personal level. The invaders are not opposed by large armies or other organized resistance, but they are fought by individual foes everywhere. Every bush, tree, rock, ditch, roof top, chimney, doorway, and window opening conceals a determined foe. This foe will fight with whatever weapons happen to be at his disposal. He will shoot with rifles, throw knives, strangle with rope, poison wells, destroy food supplies, burn down houses, and do anything else that might defeat the enemy. He is on the alert morning, noon, and night. The fight goes on day after day, week after week, month after month, and year after year. If pressed too hard he will flee to the mountains or some other inaccessible place of which Spain is full and fight on from there. When Hitler's tanks were introduced in the Spanish Civil War, the Asturian miners handled them by crawling up to them or concealing themselves somewhere along the tanks' paths and blowing them up with dynamite, an explosive with which their work had made them thoroughly familiar.

It is worth noting that the now world-famous phrase "fifth column" is a Spanish contribution. The story is that General Mola had just reached Madrid with four columns and was about to begin the long siege of that city. A newspaperman asked the General what he thought of his chances for a quick victory, and the General made an optimistic reply to the effect that five columns were an adequate force to do the job. "But General," said the newspaperman, "I don't see but four columns. Where is the fifth column?" The story is that General Mola answered by pointing to Madrid and saying that it was already inside the city. It seems, however, that the defenders of Madrid were aware of this too, for they carried out a house to house canvass systematically eliminating all suspects and the siege turned out to be a very long one.

It is clear that the only consistently small thing about such a war is that there are no large armies locked in a series of large-scale battles, although a number of spectacular sieges like the siege of Toledo are likely to occur. Nevertheless, the guerrilla can be a very terrible form of war. It is apt to produce a disheartening impression of standing still and getting nowhere because it has no true beginning, middle, or end. The invaders find that a ceaseless struggle against an unseen foe is a harrowing business and that it is acutely disconcerting to win battles that don't settle anything and most of all to go down in a defeat paved with victories.

28.

The normal way in which the Spaniard resists the authority of a government which he regards as illegitimate is the more passive one of alienation, much as though he had passed his own personal ordinance of secession. He saves the guerrilla for the more blatant cases of illegitimacy. Some of them arise because the government misuses or abuses its powers, although it came into possession of these powers legitimately. This is what happened under Charles V and Ferdinand VII. Or it may be that the government had no valid title to its power, as was true of Napoleon's brother, Joseph. The whole idea of legitimacy is of very great importance in Spain and coincides neatly with the medieval doctrine of tyrannicide with its distinction between tyranny *ab exercitio* and tyranny *ab initio*. It is noteworthy that it was a Spaniard, Father Mariana, who gave the doctrine its most extensive elaboration and carried it to such fine points that he approved the stabbing of a tyrant with a knife but he did not approve of poisoning because the tyrant himself would have to make the fatal gesture, thereby becoming guilty of the mortal sin of taking his own life and condemning his soul to eternal damnation. It was on a point of legitimacy that the Spaniards in America first separated themselves from Spain because they would not acknowledge Joseph's right to the crown. It is true that they later sought to ground their independence on the broader foundation of natural rights, but the original separation was based on their rejection of the wearer of the crown rather than the crown itself. In view of this innate respect for legitimacy, most of those who have aspired to rule Spain have gone to considerable trouble trying to establish a valid claim, but the attempt has not always been successful. General Franco was one of those who failed, and he would not be ruling Spain today had he had to depend on purely Spanish support without the overwhelming intervention of German and Italian military force.

It is the underlying assumption no less than the mode of

fighting which makes the guerrilla an intrinsically Spanish expression of personalism. When individuals resort to guerrilla tactics, it means that they are putting their ultimate reliance on themselves. Whether or not they distrust large human organizations, the fact is obvious that they are unwilling to rely on them for their personal security and, further still, that they are not in the habit of relying on them. The guerrilla, therefore, is the antithesis of collective security. Guerrilla fighters may have allies, partners, and comrades, but not commanders or superior officers. They practice on the personal level the isolationist principles of Washington and Jefferson. Considering the state as a permanent alliance among individuals for certain purposes, their antistate bias is the living embodiment of Washington's warning against permanent alliances. Their dislike for anything that entangles is such that the guerrilla could be considered as a defensive war waged by associated rather than allied powers in which individuals adopt for themselves the general position of the United States during World War I.

One effect of these underlying assumptions and attitudes is to blur the borderline between guerrilla and banditry if not actually to obliterate the distinction itself in a good many cases. The difference is mostly one of degree, and it becomes a difference in kind when the forcible defiance of authority is motivated by an unworthy cause and takes place under conditions that are not honorable. In other words, although every guerrilla fighter is an outlaw, not every outlaw is a guerrilla fighter. It is perhaps not an overstatement to say that in Spanish history most outlaws have been guerrilla fighters. At any rate, enough of them have been to color the whole Spanish and Spanish American attitude toward bandits. Where else but in the Hispanic world would one find a tendency to treat "bandit" and "revolutionist" as synonymous terms and to suppose that an outlaw might be an honorable man? We must not assume, as we too easily do, that what is true in our country is necessarily true elsewhere. The typical gangster is definitely not a Spaniard. He is an indigenous American type. For one thing, he is a businessman out to make money and engaged in activities that are prohibited by the law. Even the criterion of legality does not differentiate him perfectly from other businessmen, however, because the legality of "legitimate" business is sometimes the thinnest technicality and the animating spirit is generally the same. A more significant difference, perhaps, is the fact that gangs are not incorporated and hence must operate without benefit of limited liability. Moreover, the gang is an association of persons who are emphatically not free but are ruled and held together by terror. The Spanish bandit, on the other hand, is much more likely to be a politician and could hardly be described as a businessman even though he might be taking in a good deal of money in the form of bribes or other illegally gotten income. His band is more in the nature of an association of free and equal men who cooperate with each other from choice in their common fight against society, and he is more apt to ride on horseback openly than to drive a car behind drawn shades under the cover of darkness. The traditional Spanish and Spanish American "bandit" is somebody like the Mexican Pancho Villa or the Nicaraguan Sandino, but not like our John Dillinger. The thing which makes a man "public enemy number one" in the Hispanic world is usually not the violation of the laws against murder and theft but adherence to the wrong political party.

IN the realm of intellectual culture, it is the accepted thing to say that the Spanish are a Latin people. Much evidence can be brought in to support this idea, most of it being of the very obvious variety. Spanish is a language clearly derived from Latin and therefore closely related to French and Italian. Spanish law is based on the Roman. Educated Spaniards are thoroughly grounded in the classical literature of ancient Rome, some of whose luminaries like Seneca were themselves Spaniards. Many Spanish towns were originally founded by the Romans and the country is full of reminders of Roman civilization such as the aqueduct still being used in Segovia. It is also true that there has always been a close and continuous cultural contact between France and Spain. The same literary schools of thought have flourished on both sides of the Pyrenees. A writer like Blasco Ibañez, for example, was so profoundly influenced by France that some of his novels read like a French novel written with Spanish words. On the other hand, writers like Alarcón and Azorín are far more indigenous as anyone who tries a little translating will immediately discover. One finds in Spain the same liking for general ideas, the same emphasis on good form, the same technique of developing a theme, the same bent for deductive reasoning, the same tendency to think about politics in terms of doctrine that one does in France.

Nevertheless, all these evidences of a Latin culture and these similarities to the French should be weighed with great caution. True though they are, these things have been naturalized and therefore altered by receiving the unmistakable imprint of Spanish national character. A good example of this is the tendency to think about politics in doctrinal terms. A Spanish socialist is a man who believes in socialism, and to him socialism is first and foremost a system of doctrines. He is nothing like the English socialist to whom socialism means primarily allegiance to a party organization which endorses a mild socialist program ("program" describes it better than "principles") but is called a Labour Party. This sort of thing is as difficult for him to understand and as unattractive as it would be for a Frenchman. But whereas the Frenchman would look upon it as an instance of shoddy thinking by someone deficient in power of abstraction, the Spaniard would be more likely to see it as a bit of cowardice by a man who is afraid to fly his true colors and fight for what he believes. British socialism is typically English in that it is a bundle of compromises. The Englishman would probably not mind it were someone to tell him so, because he has no distaste for the word "compromise." On the contrary, to him it means the sensible adjustments which a mature person has learned to make in a world of give and take. It is quite otherwise with the Spaniard. In his eyes, a compromise is a deliberate betrayal of principle. The least unfavorable interpretation he could be expected to put upon it would be to call it a form of mere expediency or opportunism. It is a dishonorable business either way. What separates him from the Frenchman is something else again. The French differentiate between a principle and the person who believes in it. The Spanish do not, for they cannot conceive a principle apart from a person.

It is this inability to differentiate between them which imparts to Spain's Latin culture its distinctively Spanish quality. It accounts for several of the most striking characteristics of Spanish life. One of these is the co-existence in one person of two opposite extremes: a realism which puts color and substance in ideals and gives them a tangible if not earthy quality, and an idealism which lifts even the commonplace into a higher realm and makes the world of facts seem translucent like the paper on a Japanese lantern. Another way to express it would be to say that there is in every Spaniard something of

Sancho Panza and something of Don Quixote. It will be recalled that Sancho Panza was the one who saw everything in material and matter of fact terms whereas Don Quixote was always spiritualizing everything—windmills, inns, his broken-down horse Rocinante. Sancho Panza had the common sense and Don Quixote had the idealism.

Closely connected with this dualism which dwells deep in most Spaniards is another trait which is never or very seldom found among other nations, namely, the fusion of military and religious spirits. The *Conquistador* is very apt to be some kind of a missionary as well, and the combination of the two spells crusader. It takes a cause to arouse the Spaniard from his usual lethargy in matters political, but when it comes he will fight for it with heroism and prefer to die with drums beating and flags flying rather than to make the slightest concession even though it might save his life. Our lack of sympathy for this type of behavior shows through in our likely comment that this is the quixotic in him ("quixotic" being used as a synonym for "fool"). This Spanish attitude toward life is partly the consequence of refusing to separate person and principle since it is impossible to attack one without also attacking the other and the survival of the principle hinges on that of the person. It is also partly the result of history. The idea that principles are something to be fought for would come naturally to a people who had fought for the Catholic faith against the Moors for many centuries. When Ortega y Gasset said that a mass of people becomes a nation only when they have discovered and undertaken a mission, he was proving himself a true son of Spain.

This interpenetration of the material and the ideal, as also that of the military and the religious, is manifested in many different ways. However, if one were to name the city in which it is most obvious and complete, it would surely be the Castilian city of Ávila. It was the home of Saint Theresa of Jesus, one of the most mystical figures in the history of the

34. Catholic church and yet, for all her visions and other-world-liness, she was a great organizing force with a talent for government. It is also the most famous walled city in Spain and has no counterpart in the world except for the French city of Carcassonne. The wall is a huge and well-preserved structure built with big chunks of rock linking together a succession of massive bastions spaced at regular intervals and encircling the whole city. The home of one of the world's most mystical saints is also the world's most impressive and greatest medieval fortress. But the supreme manifestation (in the sense of materialization) of the fusion of military and religious elements is to be found in the cathedral of Ávila because the city's great protective wall forms a part of the cathedral itself so that the cathedral is an integral link in the city's defenses. Nowhere else in the world could one find a more arresting example of this fusion in spirit duplicated in this architectural fusion of rock serving simultaneously in a single structure the worship of God with the defense of man.

Spanish realism is the imperious assertion of spirit in matter. When the Spaniards represent Christ on the Cross in one of their churches, it is no serene seraphic being with a purely symbolic significance that they offer to the public. A symbol, let us note in passing, is an object which stands for a great value (religious truth in this instance) and whose meaning is fixed by conventional agreement rather than by anything in the object itself. It is something ideational rather than descriptive or graphic. But the Spanish attitude is this: why put up a symbol with an arbitrarily ascribed meaning when human art can make that meaning practically speak for itself? The Spanish Christ, therefore, is startlingly real: his blood is meant to look like blood and the agony reflected in his face is as genuine as the artist can make it. As Unamuno pointed out in an essay on the Spanish Christ in a language whose vividness and force are an example of the very thing he is describing, the representation of reality in this raw, unshaded, uncompromising, and violent way makes no concession to human weakness and causes many foreigners to recoil from it with horror and disgust. It is true that Christ suffered agony on the cross, these foreigners say, but there is no excuse for carrying realism to this shocking extreme and we can't see why the worshipper should be made to suffer too. The Spaniard, however, does think that the worshipper needs to suffer if he is to understand the meaning of Christ's sacrifice, and he wants no substitutes or abridged editions.

The issue is no different in the case of bullfighting. This national sport is almost always beyond the comprehension of the non-Spanish peoples and has done much to popularize the notion that the Spanish are a cruel and sadistic people. It is well to remember, however, that all sports belong to that category of activities that provide relaxation and recreation. There is provision for these things in every country, for they answer a deep and universal human need. There are many ways of satisfying this need, of course, and sports are only one among several. The distinctive thing about sports is that they always involve a contest of some sort whose appeal is derived from four component elements: (1) a struggle in the sense of skilled and purposeful effort; (2) something at stake, whether it is prestige or money or some other value worth having; (3) risk involving both gain and loss; (4) the pageantry which is associated with the contest or actually intermingled with it. Now this breakdown of sports into their component elements and their relation to the social function of relaxation and recreation can be applied to bullfighting and thereby made to bring out the significance of that sport in Spanish life.

The element of struggle in bullfighting is particularly strong and varied. It calls for cool nerves, great physical stamina, manifold and complex skills, and a great deal of resourcefulness. Even our own national sport of football doesn't make such exacting demands upon the players, nor does it call for as much discriminating understanding on the part of the audience to follow what is going on. Moreover, it is a cut-and-dried affair in comparison to bullfighting. On the second point, no argument is needed to establish the fact that the stakes in bullfighting are very high—perhaps as high as it is possible to make them. It is no question of money, prestige, or position. Those things are present but they are completely overshadowed by the central fact that what is at stake is life itself: the life of the horses, the bulls, and the bullfighters. If Nietzsche was right in asserting that the really great and free spirits of mankind are those who are willing to play dice with death, then the Spaniards would get a very high rating. On the third point, it is enough to mention that in bullfighting the element of risk is at a maximum. The shedding of blood that goes on is a dramatic reminder that the bullfighters are taking a chance on losing their lives and the demonstrations of the huge crowd are an equally spectacular reminder of what the bullfighters stand to gain. On the last and fourth point, even those people who are horrified by bullfighting admit that it is probably unequalled in brilliance, splendor, impressiveness, and magnitude by any public show or spectacle in the modern world. The assembled multitude is truly a sight to behold!

The same stark realism which makes the Spaniards spare no feelings when they put Christ on the cross in their churches also makes them put on a contest that is so intense that it is really a combat. They want no sham fight and no substitutes, and the experience they desire is the real and not the vicarious one. The presence of physical danger and the shedding of blood make the contest indisputably real. It is essential to note, too, who the contestants are: man and beast. It means that man with his limited physical strength and his great native intelligence and acquired skill is pitted against a brute of enormous physical strength and low intelligence, though not without a dangerous kind of cunning. That aspect of the sport is bound to have the strongest possible grip over the emotions and the interest of any human audience, a grip incomparably greater than any which the rivalry between "home team" and "visiting team" could produce. The antithesis between man and beast is so basic that it will always steal the show from the one between "we" and "they." These various aspects of bullfighting have their roots deep in Spanish life. Bullfighting is the national sport because it symbolizes the whole conception the Spaniards have of existence: a personal combat between the human as embodied in a man and the inhuman and subhuman as represented by the bull. Both man and bull are equally flesh and blood, so there can be no question of a sham fight between ghosts, abstract and bloodless entities, disembodied myths, impersonal causes, or depersonalized "historical forces." This is the basic pattern. History will change the *dramatis personae* but not the drama itself. The bullfighter symbolizes the Cid Campeador who fought to drive out the infidels, the inquisitor who fought to clear the country of heretics, the *Conquistador* who set out to subjugate a continent, Ignatius Loyola who organized the Company of Jesus and trained its members with spiritual exercises for a spiritual combat to reconquer the obviously tangible territories of Protestant Europe. The bull symbolizes the enemy, inhuman, though sometimes in human form, and always personal. He is the infidel Moor but not paganism, the heretic but not heresy, the Spanish Jew but not Judaism, the fascist invader but not "un-Spanish" doctrines. When the apologists for General Franco's rebellion waved the red flag and screamed their loud denunciations of the "Red threat," most Spaniards were not fooled. They were too accustomed to real fights to be taken in by a fake one. They could see no rampant Communists overrunning the country, but German and Italian fascists driving tanks and flying planes to shoot Spaniards and destroy Spanish towns they could and did see. If they saw a Red Menace anywhere, it was the red blood of their Basque countrymen shed by the hands of their historic enemy the Moors murdering Catholics for the self-designated champion of Catholicism.

The Basques, who are staunch conservatives, militant national-ists, and ardent Catholics, thought that this blood was all the evidence they needed to fight on the side of the supposedly "Red" Loyalist Government. And who can rightfully say now, after the horrible years that have elapsed since that time, that they were wrong? Besides, there was an enormous insult im-plied in a very subtle manner when the fascists waved a red flag to divert the Spanish people from their real enemy, for that is precisely the technique which the matador uses in fight-ing the bull. This supreme insult of identifying the Spanish people with everything inhuman and subhuman that the bull symbolizes was one of those unintentional but profoundly re-vealing slips which the psychoanalysts have taught us to under-stand, for it depicted with perfect accuracy the unfathomable contempt which the fascists everywhere have for the masses.

Spanish Expansion: Political Sovereignty vs. Cultural Sovereignty

THE national genius of Spain has been manifested with especial brilliancy in one of the world's really great ac-complishments, and yet we seldom take notice of it although it fairly stares us in the face. That accomplishment is the amazing spread and iron grip of Spanish culture and civilization over two continents and a scattering of other distant places. It is probable that a persistent anti-Spanish prejudice inherited from our British ancestors has had a lot to do with our blindness, for we have never done justice to Spain's record in dealing with alien peoples. That record shows that a small number of Spaniards acting very largely on their own won for their country most of one continent, an important part of another, and a number of remote islands in the Pacific. Furthermore, it is to be observed that most of these areas were not semivacant like those of British America but were thickly settled by native populations heavily outnumbering their conquerors. Nor was this alien mass composed of backward and undeveloped peoples like the Iroquois, Algonquins, Seminoles, Cherokees, and other North American Indians. The Aztecs of Mexico and the Incas of Peru had attained a high degree of civilization, and it is a well-known fact that the more advanced a nation is, the more difficult its assimilation by another nation is going to be. Yet, in spite of these difficulties, these native peoples everywhere have adopted the language and culture of Spain. The military conquest of some of these was a great achievement, but to conquer them spiritually and culturally was an even greater one. Even in the Philippines, far removed as they are from Spain and other Spanish possessions, Spanish civilization has taken a hold over the natives and shown the most amazing vitality. It has continued to exist intact and strong, surviving nearly fifty years of American rule. When we gave the Filipinos their independence, it was to Spanish-speaking leaders with Spanish names like Manuel Quezón, Sergio Osmeña, Carlos Romulo, and Manuel Roxas that we turned over the reins. The Japanese had to do the same when they set up their puppet government by choosing more Filipinos with Spanish names like José Laurel. When it comes to implanting one's own culture and civilization in a people of completely alien race and background, there isn't in the French, British, and Dutch possessions in southeastern Asia anything that can compare with the Spanish accomplishments in the islands of the Pacific or in the Americas. It is true that a Hindu leader like Nehru has made anti-English speeches in English before the Indian Nationalist Congress, but that was the necessity of being understood in a multilingual gathering that imposed the use of English and it was nonetheless a foreign tongue. When a full-blooded Mexican Indian by the thoroughly Spanish name of Benito Juarez rose to the highest position of leadership in his country, he too used the language of the nation which had once subjugated his ancestors, but Spanish was his own language in public as in private.

Once these notable accomplishments of Spain are recognized, it is impossible not to wonder what could have brought them about. There are good grounds for believing that Spanish personalism was mainly responsible. When the Spaniards established large plantations and other enterprises in the Americas, they came over personally. It is true that there was much exploitation associated with it, but it would be wrong to suppose that it makes no difference whether exploitation is of the personal or absentee variety. Be it ever so cruel and inequitable, personal exploitation is much more likely to be modified in practice by individual, moral, social, and religious considerations than the absentee kind. Moreover, it is very likely to improve with time in one generation if not in another, whereas the absentee kind has much less reason to change.

Another important consideration is that the Spanish colonists took the native women as wives and not as concubines, and this is the exact opposite of what those northern Europeans who moved to their colonial possessions did. Now this was quite in keeping with Spanish personalism, for marriage is the most personal relation it is possible for human beings to establish. It would not be true to say, as some people think, that taking a concubine is just as personal or even more so. The essential thing about that relationship is not who you are but what your status is. Whether a native woman is religious or irreligious, well connected or lowborn, trusting or suspicious, cultured or uncultured, socially refined or unrefined, open-minded or narrow-minded, introvertive or extrovertive, cannot be regarded as decisive. These are all personal factors, and they do not explain her status as a concubine. The only thing that does account for that status is her race, the color of her skin, the texture of her hair, or some other physical and non-personal factor beyond her control. But to choose the same native woman for a wife is much more likely to mean that she was chosen as a person and assuredly does mean that these other impersonal factors were either ignored or not allowed to make any difference. By marrying her, the Spaniard put her on a footing of equality with Spanish women if not with himself. It meant that she was raised to the conquering people's level and raised to it permanently. It meant that her children would be brought up with all the advantages and opportunities of a Spaniard instead of being left in the sorry position of the outcast or the declassed. It meant that she and her children were not to continue being the prey of native superstitions and practices but were converted to the religion of Spain.

The concern of the Spaniards for the Indians as persons or human beings was evident in a number of other ways as well. It was Spanish consciences which felt most keenly that the Indians were a moral responsibility for their conquerors. Spanish theologians and jurists felt it necessary to justify their country's rule over them and to draw the limits of that rule. Slavery was condemned and abolished in Spanish-speaking countries long before it was in the United States. Furthermore, while it is true that Spaniards were guilty of atrocities against the Aztecs in Mexico and that the Peruvian Incas never regained under Spanish rule the heights they had attained in earlier days, it is just as true that the Incas were already on the downgrade when the Spaniards found them and that Spaniards did one of the finest jobs of salvaging a subject people with the Guarania Indians in Paraguay. Justice to the Spaniards also requires that the instances of oppression so numerous in Latin America be recognized as not being based on racial discrimination but were those which might have been expected among peoples of purely Spanish stock. It was inevitable that the majority of the down-trodden would be Indians when Indians formed such an overwhelmingly large percentage of the total population of several Latin American countries, but that was due to the laws of probability and not the laws of the land. No Spanish controlled country adopted our policy of herding the Indians in reservations as if they had a plague, not even in those countries where the small percentage of Indians would have made that policy practicable. No racial discrimination withheld from the natives the educational opportunities which were made available very early in several of the Latin American countries nor blocked their way to the highest political offices. The success of the Spaniards in winning over and holding fast the allegiance of alien peoples to their culture, though not to their state, was really no accident, for is not the very essence of discrimination a failure to treat human beings as human beings, i.e., as persons? Is not the basis of native resentment and alienation everywhere the assignment of an inferior status on grounds like race which no individual ever had an opportunity to choose and cannot possibly change instead of being treated according to the things for which a person may justly be expected to take the credit or the blame? It was this deeply inherent tendency of the Spaniards to deal with individuals for what they are rather than what they happen to have, their willingness not to be stopped by the different physical features of other races but to recognize the person behind those features, and their habit of giving priority to the uniqueness of every human being in keeping with the will of God who made no two individuals identical that can explain Spain's remarkable success in the field of race relations. That success was implicit in Spanish personalism. This same personalism likewise accounts for the failures of the Spanish government. Practically nothing is left of Spanish political sovereignty over the great empire on which Charles V once boasted that the sun never set, but neither has any particle of Spanish cultural sovereignty ever been extinguished or diminished in any place where it was established.

In this respect as in a number of others, the Spanish record is the reverse of the British. The British empire is still a great political force today: a medley of heterogeneous peoples who have generally felt that the British were as wise as rulers as they often were obnoxious as individuals in social relations. The Spanish empire is gone because its people found the government unstable, inefficient, and unprogressive; but these same peoples paid the Spaniards the highest compliment any people can pay to another: they adopted as their own the language, culture, and institutions of their conquerors. Nowhere is the Wilsonian proposition that peoples are generally better than their governments truer than it is in the Hispanic world.

In a world situation like the one we are living through in which racial tensions are so threatening, we are in dire need of guidance and should welcome any contribution along that line. On the basis of the record of history, that contribution is most likely to come from those lands where the sonorous accents, melodious tones, and virile cadence of the language of Spain ring.

Spanish National Character: Problem of
American Foreign Policy

THE concern of the United States with the Hispanic world is something which is very widely recognized. It lies at the core of our traditional Monroe Doctrine, our more recent Good Neighbor Policy, our Pan-American movement, and our several efforts in direction of hemispheric defense. It is also implicit in our stake in the problem of what to do about the Franco regime in Spain. We have made progress in some of these matters but, by and large, our record is primarily the record of our mistakes. That we have gotten along as well as we have in the past we owe much more to Providence than to American statesmanship.

The most fundamental cause of our mistakes lies in the general attitude of the bulk of our people toward things Spanish. We treat the Spanish peoples in the way of a superior to his inferiors. We often act in an unfriendly manner because we think of them as "backward" peoples who have not had "the advantages" of our machine-dominated industrial civilization. We express contempt for their political institutions, we ridicule them in our movies, and many of our businessmen who have established themselves among them have been guilty of shameless exploitation. Our readiness to intervene with armed force in their internal political affairs could scarcely be justified on any other basis than naked force in view of our failure to do the same for like causes when the stronger European peoples were the offenders.

On the other hand, we have often given the Spanish peoples offense because what we thought we were doing in a friendly manner was in fact done in a patronizing and condescending manner. Now, if there is anything which all nations hate more sincerely than an outsider who comes to get all he can and contribute as little as possible it would be the outsider who comes assuming the position of a benefactor and who doesn't think there is anything worth his taking. Friendship and neighborliness are two-way relations, and to say that they are unreciprocated is to say that they don't exist. It is not really possible to make a contribution to another nation's welfare and not receive something in return because, while it is in our power to make the gift free, there is no way by which we can compel the acceptance and use of the gift. To teach anything to people from whom we are unwilling or unable to learn is utterly impracticable. The best kind—and in the long run the only effective kind—of Good Neighbor Policy would be one respecting the following conditions: (1) that what we have to contribute to the Spanish peoples is not only needed but wanted by them; (2) that we need something they are capable of contributing to us and which we are willing and able to receive. This sort of relationship cannot exist so long as we are sure that there is nothing they can teach us. That attitude is one of provincialism, and provincialism begets ignorance all around as inevitably as night follows day. Ignorance, in turn, guarantees that we shall give the wrong thing in the wrong way. International relations in this respect are no different from those between individuals. We cannot aid those we don't like because we don't know them well enough, and the reason we don't know them is that we don't like them. The foundations of knowledge are moral because knowledge presupposes learning, and learning requires incentives. The Pharisee does not learn because he thinks he has no shortcomings and hence doesn't need anything. The American diplomat who looks down upon the people to whom he is sent is unlikely to learn either because he is not looking for anything, hence he cannot help but leave his government uninformed or misinformed. Our greatest and toughest problem is to get rid of our Pharisee attitude which is as plainly evident as if we said: we thank Thee, oh God, that we are not as other men—especially these Spanish Americans over there who are dirty and dark, fight their electoral battles with bullets, don't have bathtubs, live in cities devoid of adequate sewerage facilities, ride in trains that won't run on time, can't maintain order in their bandit-ridden countries, and run around with bare feet and empty pockets and diseased bodies.

A change of attitude on our part from one of condescension

to one of sympathetic understanding based on the acceptance of the idea of reciprocity would go a long way in showing us what our mistakes have been and helping us not to repeat them in the future. One of the erroneous assumptions of our policies would emerge almost immediately. We have unconsciously assumed that political power is exclusively a matter of money and armaments. The calculation of our leaders is apparent; we shall have hemispheric security and good neighborliness if we negotiate a series of carefully placed loans in conjunction with well-planned reciprocal trade agreements with the Latin-American states and if we follow up these economic measures with the acquisition of military bases and the development of Latin-American armies with the help of United States material equipment and military supervision. If we follow these policies we shall have a greater stake in the stability and friendly character of Latin-American governments than we have had hitherto, for we wouldn't want to arm enemies. This is where we should remember that the friendship of a government does not necessarily mean that of its people, especially when we are dealing with Spanish America where friendship with one sometimes means enmity with the other.

It is high time that we should appreciate the potentialities of the cultural in politics. We must rid ourselves of the crude notion that friendship with foreign peoples, especially with Spanish Americans, can be bought or won solely in terms of economic self-interest and military security. Values are facts, and highly important facts, too, no matter what some materialists and empiricists may say about them. It is a fact, for instance, that Spanish Americans feel closely concerned with political developments in Spain and that trade statistics would be about the worst index of that concern that anybody could find. That Spain has lost practically all of her once immense empire and retains not a scrap of legal control over her former colonies in America must not blind us to the essential and permanent contribution she has made to Spanish America and the very high value which Spanish Americans set upon that contribution.

The Atlantic has made far less difference in the Spanish that is spoken by the most educated and cultured classes on either side of the ocean than it has in the English that is used by the corresponding classes in Europe and America, and the pride that our neighbors to the South take in their literary heritage is a truly Spanish pride. In the balance of international likes and dislikes, such invisible items as Cervantes, Roman Catholicism, the Roman law, the *patio,* the *pelota vasca,* and bullfighting far outweigh railroad equipment, harvesting machines, automobiles, trucks, guns, and battleships. These items are imponderables, but they are values just the same.

Spanish Americans do not evaluate these things as we do, and it helps us not one whit to say that Hispanic regard for nonmaterial values is carried to lengths which strike us as quixotic. When we talk of "winning them over," cementing "hemispheric good will," and promoting feelings of "good neighborliness," it is what they think that we must consider and not what we would think and feel in their place.

We often fail to attain our objective because we habitually underrate and sometimes altogether neglect or ignore some of the essential facts in the case, i.e., cultural facts charged with high political voltage. We are afflicted with a rigidity of spirit which prevents us from realizing that the friendship of a writer like Manuel Ugarte might win us a vastly stronger and more enduring hold over the affections of the Argentine people than anything that Juan Domingo Perón could do. It prevents us from appreciating that, when we send "good will ambassadors" to Argentina, it is better for them to know the name of Sarmiento than the price of beef. We need to learn that a few friendly stanzas by the Nicaraguan poet Rubén Darío would be worth a whole regiment of Nicaraguan dictators, that a U.S. Secretary of State praising democracy in an official speech in Montevideo would win us more good will by citing the Uruguayan José Enrique Rodó than Thomas Jefferson or Abraham Lincoln, that American visitors to Colombia would make their country more popular by showing familiarity with Bogotá's claim to be the Athens of South America than by remarking that the Colombian capital city is "a hell of a long way up," that American tourists would be more gratefully remembered in Peru for having known that the University of San Marcos in Lima is older than Harvard or that Lima women have a high reputation for beauty rather than anything pertaining to Peruvian mines.

The importance of appraising cultural facts at their true worth and therefore perceiving their political significance is illustrated by the place of France in Spanish America. Here again we are dealing with a country whose economic importance to Spanish America is negligible, but whose cultural prestige is immense. Spanish American literature has been inspired by French models, written to conform to exacting French standards of excellence, sensitive to French literary movements, and involved in French literary controversies.[2] The great jurists of Spanish America, though they write in Spanish, think like Frenchmen in terms of great legal principles and code law interpreted in the light of well-known theories and expounded in classic treatises, but not like Anglo-Saxon lawyers in terms of customary rules and court precedents,

---

[2]The Spanish novelist Juan Valera made some interesting comments on this matter in a letter to the Nicaraguan poet Rubén Darío in 1888 as follows: "I see, then, that there is no Castilian-writing author who is more French than yourself, and I say this merely to state a fact without praise or blame. In any case, I say it rather as praise. I do not like writers who have no national character, but I cannot insist that you be Nicaraguan because there neither is nor can be as yet literary history, literary school, or literary traditions in Nicaragua. Neither can I demand that you be a Spaniard in the literary sense since you aren't such in the political . . . . . This gallicism of the mind being wholly excusable, one is obligated to heap praises upon you by the handful for the perfection and depth of this gallicism, for the language you use which remains legitimately and authentically Spanish, and for the fact that you have real individuality even though you do not have national character." Juan Valera, quoted in Rubén Darío, *Obras Completas de Rubén Darío,* (Madrid: G. Hernandez y Galo Saex, n.d.), II, 12, 13.

as these are strewn in a multitude of adjudicated cases. Writers, painters, musicians, journalists, and other members of the Spanish American élite have looked to Paris, not New York, for cultural leadership. Even the wealthy Spanish Americans have preferred the beaches of Deauville and Biarritz to those of Atlantic City and Miami.

Although these facts may be something of a shock to the more self-complacent among us, the significance of France for Spanish America *politically* would be an even worse jolt. How damaging to our pride, for instance, it is to hear a Mexican (and therefore next door neighbor) say: "And to France we owe above everything else the love of liberty, that inexhaustible yearning of the Spanish American man so many times expressed in the constitutions of Mexico and Argentina . . . . ."[3] What about the Monroe Doctrine, then? Well, the truth is that our admiration for it has generally exceeded our understanding of it. The most that could be claimed for President Monroe's pronouncement and the policies that develop around it, from the Spanish American point of view at any rate, is that they preserved the independence of the Spanish American states from Europe. However, independence isn't necessarily synonymous with liberty. We are apt to think that it is because we have long and erroneously identified our own liberty with our national independence from Great Britain.

Even if we leave our Loyalists (or Tories) out of account, it is worth remembering that only some of those who fought on George Washington's side fought for liberty but that the other patriots thought they were vindicating what came to be known by the name of states' rights nearly one hundred years later. The secession of thirteen states in British America from the British Empire on grounds of British constitutional law was a cause quite distinct from the revolution of individuals in

---

[3]Mario de la Cueva, in a Prologue to *Ariel* by José Enrique Rodó, (Ediciones de la Universidad National Autonoma; Mexico: Imprenta Universitaria, 1942), p. xii.

British America fighting regardless of state lines for the Rights of Man under Natural Law against an unholy combination of American Tories, British officials, and Hessian mercenaries. An analogous dualism characterized the movement for independence in the lands south of the Rio Grande. Some Spanish Americans like Bolivar were republicans who fought for liberty, but there were other Spanish American patriots who fought for separation from Spain because they were monarchists who refused to recognize Joseph Bonaparte as the legitimate King of Spain.

The Spanish American champions of liberty and their supporters drew their inspiration mainly from France. Their movement came from the French Revolution rather than from the American Revolution, their ideals were derived from the French Declaration of the Rights of Man more than from the American Declaration of Independence, their concepts were those of Rousseau rather than Locke, and their spirit and outlook were far closer to the Encyclopedists than to the authors of *The Federalist*.

Much as many of our fellow-citizens need to be informed of these significant facts, it would be foolish to exaggerate by pushing the case to the point of ignoring the influence of the United States on Spanish American political institutions. Our Constitution, for example, has always had many admirers among our southern neighbors. There are certain features in the governments of the Spanish American republics, especially in matters of structure such as the separation of powers between executive and legislative branches, whose original models undeniably came from the United States. The surprising thing isn't that such instances exist but that they should be so few. It is also remarkable, considering the power of the United States and its proximity to many Spanish American countries, that these instances should have such limited significance (e.g., that the actual working constitution of these countries bears so much less resemblance to the U.S. Constitution than does

the written paper constitution, that the practical operation of
the separation of powers is radically different from that found
in the United States). Sometimes it is just where resemblances
are literally and textually the most exact that they are most
misleading, notably in the case of the succession to the Presidency of Vice-President Edelmiro Farrell in the Argentine Republic the real meaning of which was as alien as could be from
the succession of Vice-Presidents Calvin Coolidge and Harry
Truman to the Presidency in the United States.

The situation is much more complex than it appears to be
from almost any viewpoint one might choose to take. Of
course, in Spanish America certainly not less than elsewhere,
there are nondemocratic and antidemocratic forces at work,
forces with strong geographic and historical moorings. They
help to explain the well-known discrepancy between paper and
practice, but not entirely. Part of the explanation should be
sought in the complexity of the prodemocratic side also.
Perhaps it wouldn't be too inaccurate to suggest that there is a
primarily French political-ideological force operating with constitutional forms that are predominantly American (U.S.A.),
but that both force and forms are permeated with and modified
by the Spanish cultural heritage. Even this cautious enough
generalization is probably impaired to an extent difficult to
determine by the fact that it is pre-Marxian.

Among all these currents and crosscurrents, however,
there emerges one central truth, which is that neither the government policy nor the public opinion of the United States
has recognized the political power of the cultural in our relations with Spanish America. In appraising the items that
compose the forces that act, react, and interact among the
nations and therefore vitally affect national character within
each of the nations, we have greatly undervalued the invisible
and imponderable cultural items and overvalued the visible
military and economic items. It is this failing which is the
main cause of the misunderstandings, illusions, and mistakes

which have punctuated our dealings with the Spanish American peoples.

It is quite unnecessary, at this point, to argue the merits and demerits of the divergent ratings placed upon imponderables by Hispanic and Anglo-Saxon civilizations, considering the problem in its universal aspect. Once we make it our goal to influence foreign nations so that they will conduct themselves in the particular ways we believe are favorable to us, we have voluntarily removed ourselves from the realm of the universal and taken a position resting squarely on the home ground of those foreign nations. It should be especially easy for a pragmatically minded nation like our own to appreciate the truth that if we wish the Spanish Americans to follow certain policies and to adopt certain attitudes, we shall have to do whatever it takes to induce *Spanish Americans* to act as we want them to act and to lay our plans in conformity with the requirements of Spanish American psychology. Neither we nor other Anglo-Saxon peoples have been very pliable and adaptable in our dealings with foreign nations, and we have found the job of getting along with our southern neighbors more than usually difficult. In every case, the crux of the difficulty has been *Spanish national character* and, like the British in earlier times, we have never understood Spanish national character. Much could be said, therefore, in support of the proposition that one key—if not the master key—of our Spanish American problem lies in Spain.

There is a great deal in our history that tends to prove only too well the accuracy of these observations. Let us begin with the Monroe Doctrine. When the Holy Alliance had plans under consideration for the reconquest of the Spanish Empire, the peoples of the United States and of the Spanish American states had a number of very important things in common: (1) geographic isolation from Europe, (2) the memory among the people then living of a successful fight for independence from a European Power, (3) an interest in not being brought back to colonial status whether by force or some other way, (4) a militant republicanism. In meeting this situation, we paid no attention to the psychology of our neighbors. Our first mistake was to make a *unilateral* pronouncement. We could have gotten together with our Spanish American neighbors and made a joint declaration, since all of us had a security interest in preventing the expansion in America of the Great Powers of Europe. By neglecting this opportunity, we aroused Spanish pride against us, and that is no laughing matter to anyone who knows something about that pride. But President Monroe did consider the merits of a joint declaration—with Great Britain! The idea of warning off the Holy Alliance had originally come from the British Foreign Secretary, and it was Secretary of State John Quincy Adams who advised Monroe to act unilaterally. The historical record, therefore, shows that we had two factors to consider: (1) the good will and the pride of the Spanish American states, (2) the policy and the power of the British Government. That same record also shows that while President Monroe's declaration was issued independently of either Great Britain or the Spanish American states, we did consider acting jointly with the former but not with the latter. In other words, we were willing to weigh the claims of the British Navy but not those of Spanish American friendship. Our mistake was not to have considered the claims of both.

In addition to running afoul of Spanish pride by unnecessarily giving offense to potential friends, President Monroe and his successors made the further mistake of neglecting to make the most of the one point in the Monroe Doctrine which could have compensated for the harm done. That point was Monroe's reference to republicanism. When he proclaimed that any extension of "their system," i.e., the political and social system of the Holy Alliance, into the western hemisphere as contrary to the national interest of the United States, he raised the whole issue from the level of power politics to the higher level of political right and popular freedom. It was no longer a mere matter of not wanting the moving in of big and therefore dangerous Powers into the neighborhood; it was also a denunciation of the nature of those Powers, a declaration that their political and social system was a threat to our national existence no less than their size. It meant that we were opposed to the sovereignty of absolute monarchs ruling by divine right, flanked by aristocratic classes whose special privileges were inherited rather than earned, backed by large standing armies and strongly intrenched bureaucracies, and sanctioned by official religious establishments. But we, on the other hand, were officially committed to quite different principles concerning the nature of man and political power, principles then known by the name of republicanism. We were the political pioneers of that time, and the Spanish Americans were also. Had we stressed that aspect of the Monroe Doctrine, we might have undone the damage done to Spanish pride by its unilateral character and confronted the monarchies of Europe with the policy of the Americas instead of merely the policy of the United States. Had we done this, the Monroe Doctrine would have become truly hemispheric because of its content and in spite of the manner of its promulgation.

To stress republicanism would have appealed to the Spanish Americans as Latins for whom matters of doctrine are always immensely important and as Spaniards by supplying a common cause around which we and they could unite. It would have given us access to the controlling instincts of Spanish national character. There is too much of Don Quixote in the Spanish and Spanish American peoples for arguments based on cold-blooded strategic advantage or mere self-preservation to be very potent. You cannot get very far talking about being safe to people who want to be heroic. Neither are considerations of profit-and-loss adapted to the psychology of "economic men" likely to be appealing to people who look upon themselves as a nation of *caballeros* whose chief concern is to live and die with honor. And as for the Benthamite pleasure-and-pain psychology, it would indeed be difficult to imagine any group of people less likely to respond to it favorably than a nation whose favorite national sport is bullfighting and whose religious mystics are famous for their belief in the mortification of the flesh.

If Spaniards or their Spanish American descendants are to be aroused to action, there must be a Cause—something drawn to the scale of the immense and the magnificent, like the *Reconquista* which was fought by the Spaniards against the Moors in the name of Almighty God over a span of eight centuries under the leadership of whole dynasties. Another and nearer example, of course, would be the *Conquista* whereby a few Spaniards took possession of more than half of the New World in the name of God and King for Glory and Gold. There was gold in the undertaking, yes, but there had to be glory along with the gold to move *Conquistadores* like Pizarro and Cortés. It was a profoundly Hispanic concept which Ortega put into words when he said: "The groups that compose a State live together for something. . . . . They do not gather *to be* together, but *to do* something together."[4]

Looking back over the beginnings of our Monroe Doctrine, therefore, it is clear that our lack of understanding of the Spanish national character, which our southern neighbors inherited from their ancestors, has earned us two very costly results: (1) we have turned the full force of Spanish pride against us by acting unilaterally instead of jointly, and (2) we have failed to penetrate and therefore to arouse and to win the Spanish spirit because we did not call upon the Spanish American peoples to join us in the common cause of defending republican principles in a monarchical world.

It is unnecessary for our purpose to proceed with a detailed analysis of the subsequent history of the Monroe Doctrine. The deleterious effects on our relations with the Spanish

---

[4]José Ortega y Gasset, *España Invertebrada,* in *Obras de José Ortega y Gasset,* vol. II, (segunda edición; Madrid: Espasa-Calpe, S. A., 1936), 771.

American states of the Mexican War, the Caribbean policies of President Grant, President Theodore Roosevelt's perversion of the Monroe Doctrine (the so-called "Roosevelt Corollary") and unprincipled disregard of Colombian territorial integrity in the Panama Canal issue, President McKinley's Spanish-American War with its consequent imposition of the Platt Amendment on Cuba and annexation of Puerto Rico, President Taft's Dollar Diplomacy, President Coolidge's frequent use of the U. S. Marines and intervention in the internal affairs of Latin American states are so obvious as to be practically self-evident. After all, the friendship of nations is not to be won by exploiting them and by using armed force to perpetuate ill-gotten gains.

There is another error that we have made which cannot stand the test of a careful scrutiny, an error which goes by the name of Pan-Americanism. In general, the use of the prefix "Pan" in international relations denotes the existence of a strong feeling of unity or "belonging" that transcends state lines and has not yet achieved fulfillment in a single sovereign political organization. It signifies a strong sentimental, cultural, or racial bond among several peoples who wish for union or reunion. It applies to a powerful centripetal force which is being blocked by an existing legal order and by diplomatic arrangements. That is, for example, what Pan-Germanism and Pan-Slavism have always meant.

When we come to Pan-Americanism, however, we are facing a situation which is not even analogous. What unity one finds there is a purely external affair. The American republics may sign hemispheric treaties and sit in on so-called Pan-American conferences, but we are not justified in assuming that they feel an irresistible urge to do these things. It simply does not follow that where diplomatic representatives sit, there shall their hearts be also—much less the hearts of their constituents. The truth is that Pan-Americanism is not union but juxtaposition, and even that is the result of external compression rather than magnetic attraction. The Western Hemisphere is not one world, new or otherwise, but two worlds: the Hispanic and the Anglo-Saxon. Moreover, each of these two worlds has much closer ties with some European nations than with each other. Even geography gives the lie to the Pan-American concept, in part at least, for Argentina and Chile are farther away in mileage and traveling time from the United States than we are from England, France, and Germany. The conclusion to be drawn from these facts is that Pan-Americanism is an illusion at best and a hoax at the worst, and in neither case does it serve our national interest to cultivate it. On the contrary, it is very likely to do us serious damage by tending to confirm the dangerously false mental habit of dividing the world into three distinct compartments with three distinct foreign policies to match (the Monroe Doctrine for America, the Open Door for Asia, and Isolation for Europe).

Pan-Americanism has already had this damaging effect to a considerable extent. One instance of it is the delusion that we can encourage fascism in Spain without adversely affecting the cause of democracy which we have obligated ourselves to support in Spanish America. Nothing but the fortunes of war and divine providence kept us from reaping the consequences in Spanish America of the policy we adopted toward Marshal Pétain's Vichy regime in France during the war. Nazi propaganda was dangerous enough with the backing of the enormous and spectacularly growing Nazi power, but with the prestige of Spain, Italy, and France thrown in on the same side, the situation could have become desperate with a suddenness as startling as it would have been close. Let us not think, however, that the threat of fascism in the Americas disappeared with the removal of the Nazi menace. The fact is and remains that the continuance of the Franco regime in Spain is a massive blow to democracy in the Spanish American states not only because the prestige of the mother country is thus thrown on the side of dictatorship but also because it aligns the Roman

Catholic church against the forces of democracy in all these states. This is so because a large percentage of the Roman Catholic clergy in Spanish America is European born rather than native born and because the Catholic hierarchy naturally follows the outspokenly pro-Franco line laid down by the Vatican. General Franco would be far less dangerous if he were nothing but an individual, but it is as a symbol that he is really important, a symbol of clericalism and appeasement in whose defense people like Neville Chamberlain, Pierre Laval, and Marshal Pétain stood in the past and whose cause is now championed by others with the same idea such as Representative O'Konski and Senator Gurney. These are facts which no Pan-American curtain is going to hide from anyone, unless it be from our own people.

Another point at which Spanish national character has impinged on our foreign policies is in the matter of recognition. Our officials have quite correctly concluded that it is in the interest of the United States that our neighbors maintain not only friendly but stable governments. Unstable governments mean insecure private rights and jeopardize whatever diplomatic or political advantages may have been won by negotiation. Most Spanish American governments have been notoriously unstable, and that fact has been a source of more than annoyance and caustic remarks on our part. Our State Department has for years tried to cope with this situation through the exercise of the power of recognition and has raised this power to the status of a first-class diplomatic weapon. Recognition means more than mere ceremonial prestige. It means loans, goods, arms, and sometimes even limited military or naval assistance. We have had a difficult time, however, making up our minds about what guiding principles should control our exercise of that power. At one time or another, we have tried three different principles: (1) effective or *de facto* control, (2) constitutionality or legality, (3) degree of friendliness.

The first is the traditional international practice according to which recognition is merely a plain acceptance of the fact of effective control implying neither approval nor disapproval. The main objection to that policy when dealing with the Spanish American states is that it sometimes happens that no government is in effective control and that in many cases there is no assurance how long that control will last where it exists. This doctrine of recognition makes allowance for the fact of changes that mark a definite break in legal continuity, but it also assumes that this type of change is exceptional rather than normal and that there was a genuine continuing legal order in existence that could be broken. This assumption, however, does not fit the realities of Spanish American politics.

The second policy undertakes to grant recognition only to legally and constitutionally installed governments. It is a policy that comes naturally to American minds for whom questions of constitutionality play such an important part in domestic politics. President Wilson tried it in the hope that it would discourage violence and induce Spanish Americans seeking political power to confine themselves to legal methods. But this policy is even more hopeless than the traditional one when applied to Spanish American conditions. There is often no body of constitutional law that is equally respected by all the contestants and the constitution is apt to be more in the nature of a retroactive validation of whichever person or faction happens to have come out on top. The concept of legality is worthless as a guide for exercising the power of recognition under such circumstances as these.

The third policy frankly admits the precariousness of *de facto* control and the futility of the test of constitutionality. It simply demands that you pick among the various contestants the one that seems most friendly and malleable, and then put your chosen candidate in control by granting him recognition and withholding it from his rival or rivals. If none of the contestants is acceptable, you just enter a new one of your own.

This type of policy was used successfully (if success be defined as relative stability) by President Coolidge who chose Alvaro Obregón in preference to Adolfo de la Huerta for the Presidency of Mexico. On the other hand, this same President Coolidge used it to no purpose in Nicaragua where he sent the U. S. Marines to support President Adolfo Díaz who claimed re-election against his opponent Dr. Juan Bautista Sacasa who of course claimed the opposite. The truth was that neither man was more useful or expendable than the other, and Dr. Sacasa was elected President later on anyway. The most serious defect of this policy, however, is its unequivocally interventionist character. That one defect is certain to cost us far more in Spanish American good will generally than anything we might happen to gain in the particular country where we intervene. Needless to say, its cold-blooded Machiavellian spirit and blatantly selfish motivation make this policy objectionable on moral grounds as well.

Whatever the merits and demerits of these three recognition policies may be, the conclusion is inescapable that there can be no solution to the problem of Spanish American governmental instability in terms of recognition policies. That the problem should baffle the State Department can hardly surprise anyone, inasmuch as it has taxed the best minds in Spain and Spanish America for years. The crux of the difficulty here is nothing other than Spanish *personalismo* which the Spanish colonists brought with them to the Americas.

The Good Neighbor Policy of President Franklin D. Roosevelt is a step in the right direction in that it is considerate of Spanish pride. It also serves to dispel fear that we shall embark on imperialistic ventures again either in response to the pressure of private economic imperialisms within our borders or to considerations of military strategy. Our relinquishment of the Platt Amendment in Cuba and the refusal of the State Department to accede to the demand of certain oil interests that it resume its former rôle of bill collector for American businessmen abroad were particularly convincing in this respect. Increased expenditures for cultural propaganda are likewise an evidence of growing wisdom and enlightenment on our part in dealing with the Spanish Americans.

Nevertheless, although the Good Neighbor Policy is well calculated to achieve our objective of cultivating friendly governments in Spanish America, it does nothing toward making those governments stable. It leaves that second objective untouched because it fails to come to grips with *personalismo*. The ineffectiveness of recognition policies and of the Good Neighbor policy on this point suggests the possibility that the solution lies beyond diplomacy altogether and is constitutional rather than international in essence.

Would coalition governments be more successful (assuming that we could do something to promote them)? The idea must be dismissed almost immediately. One reason for that is institutional in character. Presidential government is one of those institutions which the Spanish American republics have borrowed from us, and true coalitions are impossible under such a system of government. Presidental government centralizes power and responsibility in the hands of a single individual, hence presidential government is necessarily personal government.

Even without institutional obstacles, however, it is doubtful that the coalition technique would work well in Spanish America. That conclusion is pretty strongly indicated by the rather long and full experience which Spain has had with that technique during the periods when her government was parliamentary. The truth is that this technique is primarily a French invention. Under French conditions, it ranges from weak minority Cabinets resting on a narrow and shifting coalition of political parties to powerful all-party or "sacred union" Cabinets resting on a stable and very broad combination of political parties approaching unanimity. This system is flexible and responsive to the demands of the French people who

normally prefer weak and impersonal government[5] for the sake
of liberty but want a powerful government with strong personal
leadership during crises for the sake of national self-preservation. Even under the second alternative, however, it is leadership and not dictatorship which is characteristic. That means
that the strong personality of the Premier is not the only strong
one in the government. Thus, the successful National Union
Ministry of Premier Poincaré formed to save the franc in 1926
contained six former Premiers.

This French coalition technique, like so many French ideas
and institutions, was transplanted into Spain but did very
poorly there. For one thing, it lost its flexibility. The Spaniards
were able to retain only the weak minority form, and even this
form worked well merely in the sense that most Spaniards do
not ordinarily rely much on government. It certainly did not
lay hold of their affection nor appeal to their imagination.
When Spain needed a strong government, the Spaniards were
unable to swing to the strong all-party "sacred union" tradition
of the French and were therefore obliged to turn to dictatorships like that of General Primo de Rivera.

The French coalition technique is not suited to the Spanish
national character, and it is *personalismo* which is most responsible for the unsuitability. The French like to think in terms of
fixed abstract principles existing independently, and the word
"objective" comes very near being synonymous with "impersonal." Principles can be subdivided into separate propositions
and corollaries, and they can also be combined into broader
generalizations. This process is perhaps nowhere better illustrated than in codes of law with their articles, sections, and
paragraphs. The Spanish, on the other hand, like to person-
alize everything and it is naturally impossible to subdivide or

---

[5]That preference is indicated in the French proverb or maxim concerning
the judiciary which says: *juge unique, juge inique.* It is also indicated by
the form in which official orders are issued. Thus, whereas we would say
"By order of John Doe, Police Commissioner," the French would leave
John Doe out and say "By order of the Commissioner of Police."

combine a person. Personality is indivisible. Political parties are uncongenial to them because they tend to circumscribe individual freedom of action and do this in the name of something less than the whole country (the word "party" comes from the Latin *pars* which means "part" or "fragment"). Political parties also require not only some subordination of individuals but collaboration and therefore compromise among individuals. The central problem here is one of legitimacy.

Neither universal suffrage nor constitutional legality has ever been sufficient to legitimize government in Spanish eyes. The most that these things can be expected to accomplish is to ward off revolution and secure passive obedience, but they will not earn passionate defense and deep-rooted allegiance. Edmund Burke's free agent theory of representation is not acceptable to Spaniards because it smacks of dictation and our own prevalent delegate theory whereby a representative "nurses" and "serves" his constituents is even more distasteful. There is no generally accepted and widely understood name for the kind of representation the peoples of Spain and Spanish America believe in—not even in their own countries. The word that would most accurately describe it would be *incarnation*.

The idea behind it is that a political leader, if he is truly representative, represents his people because of what he is personally and not because he has received the most votes, nor because he is faithfully carrying out instructions from the people, nor because he has the same interest that they have. It asserts that an official is not representative because he was elected but rather that he was elected because he was representative. A representative democratic leader, for example, is one who is democracy-made-flesh, so to speak, in that not only his opinions and convictions but his temperament, his habits, his record, and his whole manner of existence are democratic and expressed in the form most characteristic of his people's national genius. It has been said that the King of England reigns but does not rule, the President of the United States rules but does not reign, and that the President of the French Republic neither rules nor reigns. If one were to add a Spanish contribution to this collection of political aphorisms, it would run something like this: he has no right to rule who is not fit to reign.

This is a very lofty concept of representation, hence it is actualized correspondingly seldom. There is no abundance of leaders anywhere who practice what they preach and who bear the scars that prove that they were made to suffer for their integrity. There is a bit of doubting Thomas as well as Don Quixote and Sancho Panza in most Spaniards and Spanish Americans, and it is to be expected that people who do not shrink from the bleeding Christ of the Spanish churches and who enjoy the spectacle of a bullfight will not refrain from making exacting demands from their rulers. It is inevitable, too, that these demands are not going to be met often. When rulers are required to be prophets and to bear the stigmata of Christ in their persons before they can receive a real measure of authority from the governed, no clamoring mob of applicants need be expected and the seats of the mighty will be as vacant and silent as the austere and spacious Castilian countryside. We are willing to settle for less. The Hispanic peoples, however, are not, and since it is an unavoidable practical necessity that someone should rule, the consequence must be that resentment and protest against unrepresentative (i.e., unworthy) and therefore illegitimate rulers will be widespread and lead to frequent change.

We may be called upon to face situations which will test the accuracy of the preceding analysis of the problem of governmental instability in its relations to *personalismo* rather sooner than some of us think. One likely instance will occur when General Franco steps down (or is knocked down), for then the immediate problem will be to replace him and establish a stable and democratic government. It will not do to try to impose a government composed of anti-Franco exiles. Such an attempt would be foredoomed to failure. Differences of opinion are too sharp and too well known, memories are too vivid, and Spanish hates run too deep for such a solution to have any chance of success. Even if the various republican leaders could be forced to serve in a coalition government, the resulting cooperation (if any) would not be real to them nor inspiring to their followers. The participants would feel that they were asked to serve two masters, and each would be quite sure who is God and who is Mammon. Similar difficulties will some day be encountered with the eventual demise of President Perón of Argentina.

Is this problem of governmental stability insoluble? Not necessarily, provided we tear ourselves loose from old methods and old ways of thinking. Since so much of our trouble originates in the peculiarities of Spanish national character, it would make sense for us to look to some Spanish source for at least a clue to the answer. There is probably no more promising source on a question of this kind than the philosopher José Ortega y Gasset. If we apply Ortega's teachings, the first thing we must look for is a Cause: a *new* Cause great enough to kindle a sense of national mission, strong enough to dissolve old enmities, and broad enough to include the best of existing causes into a new synthesis. For Spaniards, this is the same thing as saying that a new leader of truly statesman-like dimensions must arise who embodies that cause in his person. Another requirement of Ortega's teachings is that if a movement is to have the breath of life it will have to be a growing and dynamic thing, and from this he draws the striking conclusion that nations can maintain their identity and vitality only by becoming international. In other words, growth is life and isolation is death.

The effect of this philosophy is to beam a ray of light on an otherwise gloomy situation. It suggests that the Spanish American republics will get the strong and stable governments they need if they are willing to amalgamate into a larger

political organization for a cause capable of commanding the enthusiasm and allegiance of the peoples of each of these republics. Is there such a cause? There is! That cause would be to demonstrate that a new, liberal, and more Christian civilization can be built on an interracial foundation than has been known heretofore and that the building of it will be a great step for world peace by delivering us from the dangerous situation wherein the Great Powers are too big and too few. A Hispanic Commonwealth of Nations might not be the much-talked-of Third Force, but it could at least be a third Great Power, an instigator for the United States of Europe, and the mediator between the U.S.A. and the U.S.S.R. To those who might object that this is a monumental task, the reply must be: peoples of Spanish background will respond to nothing less.

In an attempt to explain why Spain stopped expanding, Ortega y Gasset wrote the following highly significant words:

> "With the peoples of Central and South America, Spain has a common past, a common race, a common language, and yet, in spite of this, they do not together constitute one nation. Why? There is only one thing lacking which, however, is the essential one: a common future. Spain has not known how to invent a program for a joint future which could attract these zoologically kindred groups."[6]

What makes these words so significant is that they delineate what must be done in Spanish America for the sake of stability and peace. Someone else must take up the mission which Spain was unable to complete. It would be futile, of course, to suggest that our State Department announce its candidacy, but if it understands rightly what the mission is and demonstrates a willingness to give all possible assistance toward the accomplishment of that mission, our country will have done much to earn us the respect and gratitude of mankind.

---

[6]José Ortega y Gasset, *La Rebelión de las Masas, op. cit.,* p. 1261

This book has been set in Caslon Oldstyle No. 1 type
by McQuiddy Printing Company of Nashville.
The drawing on the front cover represents the Alcazar in Segovia, Spain.
It was made by Mr. H. B.
Rainey of Capper Engrav-
ing Company, Knoxville,
from a photograph
taken by Dr.
Williamson.